tHE CoNtRary KiD

written by Matt Cibula
illustrated by Brian Strassburg

Zino Press
CHILDREN'S BOOKS
Madison, Wisconsin

para mi esposa hermosa y nuestro bebé —M.C.

for Lois and Joel—B.S.

Text © 1995 by Matt Cibula.
Illustrations © 1995 by Zino Press Children's Books.
Entire contents © 1995 by Zino Press Children's Books.

Editor: Dave Schreiner; Design: Patrick Ready

The Contrary Kid is lovingly published by Zino Press Children's Books, P.O. Box 52, Madison, WI, 53701. Printed in the U.S.A.

Library of Congress Cataloging-in-Publication Data

Cibula, Matt S.

    The contrary kid / written by Matt Cibula : illustrated by Brian Strassburg

        p.   cm.

    Summary: An off-beat and unusual child does everything differently from other people but is comfortable with his unique outlook on life.

    ISBN 1-55933-177-1 (hc)

    [1. Individuality—Fiction. 2. Humorous stories. 3. Stories in rhyme.] I. Strassburg, Brian, ill. II. Title.

PZ8.3.C525Co 1995

[E]—dc20   95-20323

                                                          CIP

                                                          AC

CONTRARY. adj. 1. Totally different from what is expected. 2. 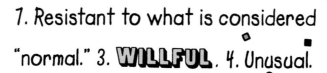Opposite. 6. Fond of wearing food. 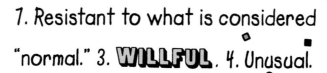 7. Resistant to what is considered "normal." 3. WILLFUL. 4. Unusual. 5. Possessing a WILD imagination. 8. A little WEIRD. 14. BUGGin' Out.

My mom calls me CONTRARY and I know just what She means—
It's like when I make Sculptures out of nasty old sardines,
Or when I take a bath in spinach soup and collard greens,
Or how I wrote this book by taking Words from magazines.

I'm the CONTRARY KiD—that means I act a little stRange,
Sometimes I get in trouble, but that doesn't mean I'll Change.

They knew I was CONTRARY from the moment I was born,
I grabbed the doctor's stethoscope and PLAYED it like a horn.
I wouldn't eat my baby food; no beets and no creamed corn,
FRIED RICE with peanut butter was my breakfast every morn.

I'm the CONTRARY KID — that's just the way I am,
I ♥ a sweet potato but I yam just what I yam.

I color all **O**utside the lines, but please don't disapprove –
They took my favorite coloring book and hung it in the **L**ouvre.
I taught the ocean how to wave and motion how to **MOVE**,
James **B**rown wrote me a letter saying, "Thank you for the groove."

I'm the **CONTRARY KID** – that's what my **m**ama said
When I came home from school one day with **p**izza on my head.

I'm really very selfish, but I'll give you all my money,

I hop around the house a lot and **roar** just like a bunny,

I'll sing the saddest song you know and still you'll think it's FUNny,

Put pepper in my cereal and brush my hair with honey.

I'm the CONTRARY KID — that's what your parents think —

They saw me jumping rope inside your family's kitchen sink.

I guess I must admit at times I act a little WEIRD –
One time I went to school wearing a big blueberry beard.
The children in my classroom Stood and Laughed and Clapped and Cheered,
We went on celebrating till the principal appeared.

I'm the CONTRARY KID – you've never seen my like before,
I run across the ceiling 'cause my mom just mopped the floor.

You ask me how I'm doing and I say "The Porcupine*."
You ask my favorite animal, I say "I'm doing fine."
You ask me "Can you Sing for me 'My Darling Clementine'?"
I say "Yes ma'am" and sing it just like Dr. Funkenstein.

I'm the CONTRARY KID — I just went swimming in the park,

I'm doing fine.....

And you'd swim too if you were being chased by that big shark.

I must admit I gave myself a **weiRDO** style of **h**air:

The **TOP** is like a triangle, the ~~bangs~~ are sort of **SQUARE**.

I think it looks unusual and full of zesty **fLAir**,

My **m**ama thinks it looks like **I** was **beat** up by a **b**ear.

I'm the **CONTRARY KiD** - but don't **c**all me a jerk,

My **FULL**-time job is *chillin'*, and it's time to go to work.

I'm sorry for my teacher 'cause I think I made her cry:
She told me two times two was four, I had to ask her WHY?
Some afternoons I'm ROWDY and some mornings I am shy,
Sometimes I want to make a chocolate caterpillar pie.

I'm the CONTRARY KID—I don't have Time to fret,
And if you do not like me, you just haven't met me yet.

I have about a million friends, we hang out 'round the clock,
'Cause I know all the animals who live around my BLOCK :
That frog is named Lumumba and that garter snake is Spock,
So if you want to hang with us let's go lift up that rock.

I'm the CONTRARY KID — let's have a ROCKIN' time.
Sometimes I'm so contrary that a line goes on and on and on and on and on and on and on and on and on and on and on and on and on and on and on and on and on until I finally decide to make it rhyme.

Last week I was an **astronaut**, I went to outer space,
The week before I DANCED Swan Lake with dignity and grace,
I think this week I'll try to run a hundred-mile race —
Or maybe I'll stay home and paint some flowers on my face.

I'm the CONTRARY KID - and that's the honest truth,
An off-beat and unusual Extraordinary youth.

I guess I am a human, but I wish I were an Ape,
I guess I'm person-flavored, but I wish that I were grape,
I guess I'm not a SUPERhero, but I wear a cape,
I also wear a mask that I made out of Masking Tape.

I'm the CONTRARY KID - they say my clothes are WiLD,
I am my own designer, I'm a fashionable child.

Now on a normal Saturday I cartwheel down the road,
I do not speak to anyone except in SECRET code,
I jump around a little and pretend that I'm a toad,
Then I go home for dinner: broccoli ice cream á la mode.

I'm the CONTRARY KID — don't be scared of me or run,
I don't mean to ALARM you, I'm just trying to have Fun.

I met the new girl in my class, her name's Taquandra Fu.

She came to school in one GREEN slipper and one PURPLE shoe.

Now even though that's not what I would wear, 'cause I like blue,

I think we're going to be good friends, 'cause she's CONTRARY too.

We're both CONTRARY KIDS—we're happy and we're smart.

To truly be contrary is a science and an art.